* * *

A Walk In The Park

* * *

A Walk In The Park

Through The Psychotherapist Mind

Dr Alberto Albeniz

ISBN: 1518640621
ISBN 13: 9781518640629

Dedicated to Aita

✳ ✳ ✳
ACKNOWLEDGEMENTS

I started to design the first drafts of this book in English. Then Joan Shenton suggested that I write them first in Spanish, in order to get closer to my thinking spirit and then translate it into English. This exercise developed a parallel creation in both languages, my native one and the one from my professional life, in which each contributed to the other.

This book has been possible thanks to the motivation and constant collaboration from my father Juanjo with the Spanish version and Joan with the English one.

I would like to express my gratitude to valuable comments from other friends like Dr Ángel Sánchez Bahillo, Dr. John Ryder, Dr. Jon Izaguirre, Rosemary Prior and specially Dr. Oscar Bosch.

TABLE OF CONTENTS

✳ ✳ ✳
INTRODUCTION

The idea and the purpose behind this book arose from learning through practice.

This is a collection of the metaphors used as support materials in my supervisions, informal talks and conferences with doctors training to be psychiatrists and with psychotherapists in Coventry.

The stories are an attempt to share the small but significant insights that the therapist gathers over the years during the dynamics of interaction.

I have always felt the need to avoid, within the strictly necessary, long and complicated theories. I have tried to extract the essential elements from theoretical concepts, setting them out in a simple and attractive way.

In my experience, and especially in the early years of practice, the one- method system of teaching, whether involving behaviour, cognitive, psychodynamic or systematic therapy, has sometimes carried with it the risk of clone-copying or imitative variations of techniques restricted to text books. In my view, an approach that regards form more important than content generates confusion. It could lead to students drawing premature conclusions about their own lack of conviction and effectiveness.

Conversely, I have found it gratifying to see how the emphasis on a more open approach initially, peppered with classical techniques, has helped many students develop their own particular style in accordance with their own personality, often involving very different kinds of modalities.

I do not wish to suggest that good psychotherapy is easy. It unquestionably requires years of dedication and study. The task of diagnosis interprets biological markers within a psychological context, and from the origins of these roots that often stem from a person's earliest development, from the family and the society that surrounded them then and surrounds them now.

Study familiarizes the psychotherapist with the different qualities of the mind, in particular the rhythms of the unconscious. When it comes to the description of the workings of nature, science has made important strides through the practice of observation and experimentation. This knowledge, when related to the human mind has, in the first instance, gone hand in hand with a sense of respect for the mind's inscrutability. Secondly, it has helped to hone the therapist's skills in aligning herself with the particular ways in which the unconscious functions, allowing a gentler fluid approach.

In spite of the extent and variety of psychological and psychotherapeutic theory, practice very often tells us that simply having knowledge of theory does not guarantee success. Theories do not explain why things happen. More often they attempt to describe processes and pose hypotheses. These, rather than being able to predict the future, serve to help us avoid too many big surprises and also to familiarize ourselves with any possible outcomes.

The psychotherapeutic encounter differs from the practice of sporadic psychiatric consultations. A continuity of relationship, at least once a week for a minimum of several months, helps create a reflective space allowing the therapist to see the patient in more of his entirety.

Sooner or later the student will arrive at her consulting room at a moment when none of the emergency tricks are working. These tactics, although ingenious, are usually put into practice in an isolated fashion and are the consequence of badly understood theories that tend to treat the patient as a mere receptacle. It is then that the clinician can no longer ignore those much-feared silences and he feels vulnerable. These are the critical "I don't know what to do now" moments.

When she has found the courage to bring these doubts to supervision, a more profound understanding takes place. This understanding leads to the recognition of the influence that the patient has over the therapist and vice-versa.

It has been very gratifying to watch the way in which many of the students begin to discover more practical and strategic ways of putting theory into practice and how they change their attitude, corroborating that they find what was put before them was neither new nor difficult. It is all within their range of comprehension. Although sometimes that comprehension remains beneath the surface during their initial superficial appraisal, by drawing on their own resources they are easily able to recognize this comprehension as intimately rooted in their own personal experience of human relationships and life events.

This comprehension within the students themselves is often a phenomenon that emerges in parallel with, or in second place with, the very same comprehension they are trying to elicit from their patients.

The metaphors in this book are separate from the real-life examples that inspired them in honour of confidentiality, brevity and simplicity. The chapters are independent of each other. In order to best understand them the reader needs to have a certain amount of therapeutic experience and, so that as with the pieces of a puzzle, she can make them fit them together in accordance with her own experience.

I hope that through these metaphorical threads I can share with the reader the spirit of the adventure and exploration on the journey with the patient and the fascination that is felt by both as the patient gradually learns acceptance of himself.

Chapter 1

VAMPIRES

The vampires' story is based on the age-old myth originating in Eastern Europe's Transylvania.

Vampires were portrayed as creatures similar to human beings who chose to live their lives in far away castles. They would wake up in the middle of the night, creep up on their victims and attack them with a bite on the neck in order to suck their blood, this being their only means of sustenance.

Vampires were always elegant, attractive, well educated, with refined manners. In some versions of the legend vampires lived very long lives, far exceeding human life expectancy. They were always of noble extraction and had personal means. These characteristics were in sharp contrast with their extreme isolation and the tumbledown state of their tenebrous mansions. The mystery surrounding them and their aristocratic airs served to deceive their victims.

Their powers of persuasion helped them in their quest to seduce, blackmail and kidnap their victims. They rarely revealed their desperate practised, becomes an open and unhurried encounter between the patient and the more remote recesses of the patient's mind. Hand in hand with this goes the ability to confront problems, getting to the heart of the matter, taking responsibility and going all out with no holds barred.

When I refer to psychotherapy as "well practised" is because not infrequently patients attend psychotherapy sessions on a whim, and are unwilling to get "to the heart of the matter".

There has to be daylight when first confronting these problems, exposing them to the light of objectivity, examination and reflection. This takes place not only in the clinic but also through other emotional avenues involving family and friends. The 'feed-back' from these relationships is crucial in order to be able to uncover aspects of the patient's thinking that would otherwise remain hidden under a cloak of fear and denial.

Not surprisingly the therapist herself can encounter that same seductive negativity in the patient-therapist arena. For example she can experience complex emotional reactions in a clinical situation that feel alien to her usual state of mind. These can be feelings of fear, attraction, and the desire to rescue the patient or simply to get away from him. She discovers how internal structures are brought into play in order to protect the pathological nest that offers nourishment to the original pain. For example the therapist can feel the need to justify herself by intellectualising or by self-praise. Only a strict process of self-monitoring of her conscience perhaps not immediately (it could take a long time) sets her back on course and makes her aware of the alienating nature of this seduction. It is only then that the patient can be helped by the therapist to detect those vampire elements in his mind not only in his own unconscious but also in that of the society that surrounds him.

Freud advocated "insight" as a way of illuminating the mind and providing a vital platform in psychoanalytical exchange. This transition of material from the unconscious to the sphere of the conscious can bring about a catalytic transformation.

There has always been a need to hunt down one's own personal vampires, and often people embark on this pursuit on their own but it can be easier and safer to do it under the guidance of a companion who is familiar with the territory and who may have been through the same experience himself.

The art of psychotherapy is far more complex that it would appear. It is based on the cumulative experience of the many who have gone before us. The study of principles helps develop techniques for the correct timing of the application of solutions that will lead to successful personal growth. Every therapist has her own favourite recipes, the major part learned and adapted and some entirely original.

In the next few chapters I shall attempt to highlight some of these ideas. I shall not be describing entire case studies but simply offering the reader a series of glimpses from which she can draw her own conclusions.

It is as if you were trying to complete a puzzle where you could decide on several different approaches. Some might start by piecing together the edges of the puzzle; others might begin with a corner. There are those who separate the pieces according to different themes or colours and others by size and shape. In this book, just as in psychotherapy, you will already know that some of the pieces of the puzzle are missing. Perhaps thanks to this, creativity becomes a necessary part of the process in order to complete the adventure embarked upon by both the patient and psychotherapist

✳ ✳ ✳

Chapter 2

IN THE PARK - PART 1

L et us imagine that a mother is taking her two year old son, Paul, to a playground in the park for the first time. The park is surrounded by a fence and has swings, slides and sea-saws, a little pond, and some benches.

Let us follow along behind the mother, Mary, who is going to intro-duce her son to some brand new adventures in the playground.

She begins by choosing a bench that will later become her favourite place and leaves her bag and coat there. Then, always remaining inside the perimeter of the fence, she takes Paul by the hand and shows him the playground equipment, giving each ride a name and letting him see how the other children are enjoying themselves. It being the first day, fifteen minutes seems more than enough time for this. On returning to the bench the mother gives Paul a hug and a sweet whilst she describes with enthusiasm the things they have just seen. In this way Paul begins to absorb these new experiences together with the need to be careful.

On a series of subsequent visits Paul gradually becomes familiar with this environment. Little by little he feels more at ease and less fearful. Then comes the critical moment when his mother decides to suggest he go down the slide. She takes care to stay close to him, holding his hand, and letting him go little by little, always watching out for his reactions.

If fear should overcome Paul, Mary would intervene prudently, reassuring him with a hug and distracting him with a strategic halt in the proceedings. Then she will push a little further. She continues with this art of letting go but at the same time keeping up a sense of mutual security combined with a sense of fun. She carries on using this reward approach until she succeeds in raising the spontaneous laughter that results from having mastered something. Paul begins to learn through play whilst his mother continues to manipulate the situation with an intelligent mixture of tact and affection, and at the same time enjoying every minute of Paul's progress.

This is why Mary now follows Paul on to all the different playground equipment from the simplest to the more complicated. She also helps him communicate with other children making him feel part of the group.

In a third phase Mary wisely moves away a little so that Paul, almost without noticing it, can become absorbed in his play and gradually forget the need to feel his mother's presence. Mary eventually goes back to the bench, always watching carefully. She leaves Paul to go on enjoying the slide, climbing the mini mountains, slipping through the ropes or playing alone on the swings.

The parallel in clinical practice is in the relationship of trust between patient and therapist. Despite the professional status of the therapist, it is perfectly natural for the patient to feel he must keep testing the therapist out, little by little. The difficulty for the patient is in his capacity to actually stay on in the presence of the therapist, to let go and to risk being psychologically naked. It is even more difficult for him to open himself up to a complete stranger who could never (nor should ever) correspond on a personal and intimate level. The patient has to learn how to place his trust in the therapist without losing his own balance whilst at the same time wrestling with an overwhelming timidity and sense of shame.

Learning the emotional language that is called upon in a clinical situation is not something to which everyone is accustomed. Both patient and therapist need to learn it together. In his consulting room, the therapist first needs to establish a secure environment and a regular pattern, perhaps in one weekly one hour session. Professionalism and a sense of security go hand in hand. Professional ethics involves not only the training needed but also the ability to inspire confidence carefully and honestly avoiding comment on the therapist's own problems or personal experience, so as not to muddy the waters in communication and to avoid confusion of roles between therapist and client. This open and receptive approach encourages the patient to explore different areas of his psyche. The comings and goings of everyday life, emotional highs and lows, disturbing impulses, the vertigos of insecurity, the stomach-churnings of panic, are all phenomena that need to be approached delicately, resolutely and with the same attention to detail with which the mother plans each step for her son in the playground.

By gradually alternating the security of closeness with a spirit of adventure spurred on by physical separation, the child gradually builds up his self confidence, giving free reign to his innate sense of curiosity which, in turn, leads him on to greater feats.

In a certain way the initial physical bond becomes transferred to a mutual visual contact between mother and son, which makes their separation easier. That constant maternal supervision begins to work by remote control and, together with a third element of fore-warning and instinctive natural concern, acts as a radar, ready to detect imminent danger. Support at a distance not only involves this radar but also certain gestures of touch. These keep up the feeling of closeness, reminding the child of the "I am here to look after you and protect you" factor.

Paul knows this. He knows that whenever danger presents itself in the shape of an obstacle or an accident, his mother is always there to take instant action. She is prepared to jump up from the bench and run towards her child. She either resolves the problem immediately or she supports Paul so that he may resolve the situation on his own or under her instructions.

The child gradually begins to take master the different pieces of equipment on the playground, the different areas there, and his relationship with other children as well as to develop his own ability to compete, hold back, or push forward. The child learns the rules and the limits of the game.

If, for example, he accidentally falls off a swing or if he hurts his leg, his self-confidence and sense of fun unravel. If that impact is considerable, Paul's confidence can be completely undermined. It is then that an automatic response sets in and he looks for the security he experienced at the very at the beginning. He goes straight back to the bench crying and asking for help in order to reactivate the restorative contact with his mother.

In moments like these, an experienced mother would never say something like "you're hopeless, you're just not up to this" or "don't you ever try that again – we'd better give this all up". On the contr. ,, she will try to contain her anxiety about her son in order to avoid panicking and she will attempt to adopt a positive attitude. She may not be able to avoid showing some signs of distress, just enough to make Paul aware that she noticed what went on, but she swiftly refocuses her efforts in a positive direction.

In a way, the reaction to the accident produces a double response from mother and son. They both waver in their confidence in one another and go back to previous phase, a re-encounter on the original bench, the symbol of stability and protection. This synchronised mutual suffering helps engender a common understanding of Paul's need of her presence and help.

Although the effects of the accident die down, recovery from it requires a step by step repeat of the whole process of the discovery of adventure that had gone on before, albeit in a shorter modified form. Starting with the short distances and minor risk- taking, combined with the mother's warnings and admonitions telling her son to be careful, until the level of competence achieved just before the accident is reached once again.

This does not mean re-learning on the basis of simple repetition. Instead, a form of spiral learning is required, taking off and coming back to the same point time after time, gaining more confidence on each sortie. This time the learning curve moves more quickly as it follows the beaten path and traces of the previously learned experiences.

The child has learned a new lesson. He now knows that he can fail and also learn from his past mistakes. He knows that an emergency system is available. This gives him a deeper sense of security and feeling of

or more seriously, falling into the water, he needs dry clothes and shoes in order to avoid catching a chill. When the water is deep the swimmer has to know how to swim because he can't touch the bottom and he has to keep his head above water in order to breathe.

The pond is an example in a microcosm of other aquatic scenes that an adult might encounter. When we get rivers and seas we need to become familiar with the currents, which, although invisible to the novice, can carry us away.

In some ways a clinical exploration of the different levels of consciousness, between the conscious and the unconscious, is like the difference between *terra firma* and the water in the pond, river or sea. The conscious mind relates to being able to discern, to recognize, to measure, to weigh up, to explore, plan and consider particular strategies – all in the light of day.

The unconscious mind is more elusive and diffused. It has different rules and a different depth, and when it is overly stimulated it becomes more difficult to explore and elucidate. It has its underground currents with their own different forces, pressures and temperatures. It has its memories, its objects from the past, its entities, its disinterred refuse and its desires – some occasionally evanescent in all their different shapes and colours - as well as its frightening creatures, fears and aversions and it amorous impulses be they sexual, creative or destructive. The unconscious has its complexes, which are difficult to capture, it has fighting monsters that scratch or create menacing circles like sharks or bite like piranhas.

Psychotherapy is a way of helping the patient not only manage himself on dry land or on the top of a mountain, but also to familiarize him with the laws of the unconscious. Therapy helps teach the patient to swim, to navigate, to snorkel and to allow himself to enjoy with more confidence the delights of the deep or the advantages of surfing along the top in a safer way. The instructor is a seasoned mariner with respect for the waters, the winds, the currents and the tides, knowing how to steer clear of danger and how to take full advantage of the mysteries surrounding the different elements he encounters. She is a sailor who knows how to hold breath in his lungs long enough to be able to dive into the depths of the unconscious for as long as is necessary.

When it comes to water, more so than in the example on dry land of the park, the explorer needs the experience and guidance of the mariner who has navigated those waters before.

Up to a point, the mother in our example in the park fulfils, the first steps undertaken by the mariner guide. The central figure of attachment extends gradually into the lives of others, the father, the grandfather, the nanny, the brothers, other family members, teachers and friends in general. If the first experience of attachment is a good one it makes it easier for the child to trust other figures that will appear later in life. These may include, at a later stage, friends, employers, spiritual leaders, favourite authors, philosophers and also other generations – children and grandchildren. All of them help a person explore the world in all its diversity. The areas of exploration are shared out amongst these figures of attachment each taking on specific tasks. One of the richest of these relationships is that between husband and wife. This intimate relationship between couples creates an invitation to discover unimagined territories, especially at the emotional level whether conscious or unconscious.

In time, Paul begins to take on other challenges. His mother had forbidden him to climb some trees at the bottom of the park because this would obstruct Mary's visual control. But one day his natural curiosity pushes him in the direction of this unknown territory. He starts by hiding behind a tree trunk for a few seconds.

What is the significance of this moment?

Paul and his mother experience a new feeling of anxiety based on the interruption of the bond of eye contact they had between them. Because this link between them has been broken Paul feels an unexpected surge of insecurity. The only thing to do is to repair the link. He comes out of his hiding place and checks to see that his mother is still looking his way from the bench. At the same time the mother had also felt the anxiety caused by the interruption. For just a moment she is not quite sure where Paul is. If this separation should last longer than expected, we can imagine the mother's response. She would get up from the bench, look for her son, make sure he is all right and return to the bench. This would reduce her anxiety, and create a sense of mutual relief accompanied by a smile from both of them. The mother might also tell her son off in an attempt to re-enforce the pressure of all things that are forbidden with words like, "I've told you not to do that", "don't you dare do that again because you could get hurt, etc."

But, true to life, in spite of the utterly understandable reactions the day before, Paul is tempted to repeat the scene the next day. So separation anxiety and fear of being reprimanded are overtaken by the desire to advance into that unknown territory, combined with the positive memory of having after all survived yesterday's feat in the end.

This second time he succeeds in hiding behind the tree for a little longer. One can imagine how the whole cycle is repeated, for a little longer each time. He enjoys the sense of fear followed by relief, hugs and smiles from his mother and also the fact that each time he repeats the scene he overcomes his fears.

Paradoxically, reward and punishment when functioning in unison promote exploration with certain touches of precaution. It is a double game that he's been familiar with since he was a baby when his mother used to hide behind the cot and reappear saying "cooed" with smiles and kisses. But this time he is the one that has to take the initiative.

The next stage results in Paul's increasing the time of separation and at the same time increasing the risk takes place by perhaps climbing the tree without worrying too much about falling down and without minding the telling off from his mother for having broken the pre-arranged rules or for having torn his trousers. The excitement of discovery and the inner feeling of being able to master a situation provide advantages that stake precedence over any feeling of risk or anxiety. Paul learns, unconsciously that self- confidence is achieved when he confronts his limitations slowly and progressively, and when he learns to live with his temporary states of insecurity instead of avoiding them.

On closer observation we discover that when Paul jumps behind the tree, this apparent break in the attachment between mother and son is not quite what it would appear seem on the surface. The external attachment between mother and son begins historically with the umbilical cord. Gradually this is replaced with other more sophisticated and less tangible cords.

What occurs in the first moment of separation, in the example of hiding behind the tree, is that together with the external visual attachment an internal mental representation has gradually been developing. This mental attachment is symbolic of the external attachment,

forgiveness and reparation, is done on the firm basis that these transitional objects cannot bite back as they have no memory.

In Paul's case - now grown up and traveling the world - a simple photograph of his mother, his house, the place where he was born, or of his friends will suffice in moments of stress to provide that essential access to the internal bond and revive those engraved images and memories from the distant past.

It could be a photograph or it could equally be a childhood song, a lullaby, a pop song, a place or symbolic objects, certain habits, domestic rituals or even celebrations and anniversaries.

The marvel is that these transitional objects develop in a space peculiar to them and can develop almost magical properties. As diplomatic ambassadors they enjoy certain immunity. They operate in neutral protected territory that embraces both worlds – the internal and the external. The territory is neither completely external nor internal and at the same time, is an extension of the two, occupying space as it does, in both of them.

This is the space of abstraction and of the imagination. This is the territory of the art, of culture and of spirituality. Each one, external and internal, is mediated through symbols (transitional objects themselves) which provide a further intangible dimension. For example a painting or a poem can generate concrete external stimuli as well as powerful internal evocations.

This transitional space means that its boundaries are permeable. The internal world develops principally from images derived from the external world. Conversely, the external world is also modulated to a certain extent by the internal world. Paul ends up understanding that what is going on around him is the key in relation to what is going on inside him. It is as if Paul could turn into a bear tamer in a circus because his transitional object was Winnie the Pooh or Yogi Bear – a cycle fed by the past.

This interaction also helps with the transition to a third evolutionary stage – the first being the omnipotent child, the second being the transition from self-centredness to a duality that is polarized between the 'I' (the child) and the 'non-I' (the mother), and now we have reached the third stage. This stage stems from the attachment between mother and child which by creating an intermediary space, one of transition, of negotiation, of creativity and communication benefits both of them. This intermediary space allows, through a process of positive feedback, for a gradual transformation of their external and internal worlds.

This is the beginning of the concept of society, a third space that connects the individual with the rest of existence.

Chapter 4

* * *

IN THE PARK – PART 3
AY! MUMMY'S GONE

Until now we have been exploring an ideal situation with an ideal mother and child and an appropriate setting with the just the usual obstacles that crop up in a normal uncomplicated life. In this part we shall explore events when these ideal circumstances become more complicated or distorted.

What happens when the bond between mother and child is severed, be it by accident or by design?

In order to help analyse the situation I invite the reader to return to the scene in the park.

A few months go by and Paul returns to the park with his mother to play on the swings. He has now made friends with some of his playground companions. They are small boys like him and everything is more fun than ever. The mother sits on her favourite bench with a book or a sock to darn, always keeping a watchful eye on her son. She too has made friends with some of the mothers who share the same bench with her. They exchange chitchat about their problems, concerns and the behaviour of their children in the park or at home.

One day something normal but different takes place. Paul's mother Mary needs to go to the bathroom urgently. There's a public lavatory very close by and before getting up from the bench she asks the friend sitting next to her, Luisa, to keep an eye on her son.

But, as luck would have it, although Paul appears to be absorbed in his games, he unexpectedly looks up and notices his mother's absence, which lasts about three minutes.

His first reaction is to drop everything and start looking for her, racing frantically from one place to another. He finds only Luisa on the bench. She tries to calm him down explaining that Mary needed to go to the bathroom for a few moments and that she would soon be back. But instead of calming him down, this causes Paul to fly into a paddy, bursting into tears of rage because he thinks he has been abandoned. Even when his mother comes back his fury continues unabated. He does not, or will not, understand that his mother has her own needs and her own independence. All he can think is that he has been abandoned. This is the cause of his fury against his mother as he watches all the previous structures of relationship with her collapse.

In an attempt to find some kind of reason for this sudden rupture Paul might think his mother either does not love him or that he has done something wrong. So Paul could blame himself and believe this separation is his punishment. All this builds up so quickly in his young mind that he cannot make sense of it all. His stress level builds more than he can bear and when mother returns, anger bursts out.

A mother who cannot understand the reasons behind such an outburst would react with a rebuke because of the embarrassment she is being put through and her feelings of "what will my friends be thinking?". She might also simply ignore her son's behaviour, leaving him alone until he calmed down. However, these approaches would only succeed in reinforcing the child's sense of guilt and feeling of worthlessness. If his mother was incapable of coping with the shame of what had gone on, all the more reason for him not to cope either.

But because Mary understands the situation, she bears with the tearful outburst for as long as it lasts without stooping to easy rejection or reprisal. Once the storm has passed she remains watchful, biding her time and waiting for the right moment. This is when the fury begins to subside and the child's desperation makes him receptive to a strong embrace. This embrace not only comforts the child but it serves to dissolve his negative thoughts, repairing the ruptured link and the harm caused by the storm that has now passed.

Mary is a good mother who is sure of herself and who in spite of inwardly suffering her son's pain, is capable of absorbing it, not just superficially, but for what it is. Being able to tolerate adversity is the greatest example of maturity. This quality is transmitted from mother to son who, as circumstances repeat themselves, assimilates it and begins to develop his own emotional flexibility.

Let us just imagine that the situation repeats itself the following day. The mother needs to excuse herself in order to go to the bathroom. She takes the same precautions as the time before with her friend

Luisa and goes off. This time, for whatever reason, she takes twice as long, six minutes. Paul soon notices her absence.

The first three minutes are very much a repeat of yesterday's performance. During this time Luisa notices that Paul's fury gradually turns to sadness and he then begins to weep inconsolably burying himself in the folds of her (Luisa's) skirt. His mother is not to be found. The previous day Paul had associated his outburst of anger with the timing of his mother coming back and the resolution of the incident. This time his fury is not only of no avail, rather it is exhausted, giving way to a sense of loneliness and desolation.

At last his mother returns to the bench. Paul overwhelmed with sorrow and weeping takes a while to notice her. If Mary were not so mature and well balanced, she would not be able to bear Paul's anguish and might have reproached him for his weakness, thus increasing the lack of understanding between them and the sense of mutual rejection and isolation.

The more Mary is capable of containing her own feelings of dismay the more receptive she is towards her son's plight. Thus her thoughts revolve around Paul's needs and consoling his sense of aloneness and desperation. She is capable of being there for him. She is able actively to hug Paul – a physical gesture that acts as a bridge firstly containing the sorrow and then the fury, reactivating the bond between mother and son. As a consequence, an emotional calm is established allowing a stronger mutual emotional flexibility to emerge.

Let us imagine the same situation yet again on another day. This time, the bathroom was occupied so the mother takes nine minutes to return to the bench.

What does Luisa observe in Paul's reactions this time? The first six minutes were almost identical to those of the previous day. But after that, a change takes place. Luisa notices something different after the fury has turned to sorrow and he has once again sought refuge among the folds of her skirt. He seems inconsolable in spite of all her efforts to cheer him up. The initial phase of protest is followed by a feeling loss and desolation but when these six minutes are over Paul stops crying. Maybe he is just tired of crying as if realizing that even when he feels alone, expressing his feelings doesn't succeed in bringing his mother back to comfort him. It is as though he has decided that the most practical thing is just to get on with it. Luisa then notices that Paul gets up, pulls himself together and, as if nothing has happened, goes back to his games in the playground.

When his mother returns she sees a child who seems to be fine and as calm as he was when she left him. Luisa tells her what has happened.

A less experienced mother might say to herself, "Paul has sorted things out by himself; best to leave him alone. Good. It looks as though Paul can take care of himself now, just like a grown-up."

But Mary is an experienced mother and her intuition tells her that despite appearances her son is not at all well. So she goes up to him just where he is. The child's reaction is to ignore her as though he were saying to himself, "You pushed me away. You abandoned me. You don't need me so I don't need you either. What point is there in trusting you when you ditch me when I least expect it? It's better to be alone than to be badly looked after or risk disappointment again. Three cheers for independence!".

Of course this silent act of rejection stems from unmet needs and wounded feelings.

A good mother is able to see through this and puts up with this temporary period of rejection; this attitude which is saying, "I don't need you. Leave me alone". In spite of her understanding of the situation she still feels the sting of rejection, of being pushed away and not needed.

These feelings are an immediate reflection of the child's feelings. We might imagine that the child is unwittingly projecting his feelings of discomfort onto his mother. She absorbs them and can't ignore them. She may be a little confused at first as to the origin of these feelings, because she might wrongly identify them as feelings emanating from her. The tension of the moment does not allow her to properly gauge the real origin of these feelings. But once she has regained her equilibrium, she can see where these feelings are coming from. They are coming from Paul. This, in its way, is one of the most primitive forms of communication.

She has simply acted as an intermediary in a chain of communication. Paul experiences strong and raw emotions that he can't assimilate. They overwhelm him and make him feel alone in face of imminent danger. Unconsciously he wants to get rid of these emotions as fast as he can so he passes them on to the nearest person, to Mary. She receives them, allowing Paul the chance not to totally reject them as useless. She is capable of holding on to these emotions, even to digest them, taking the initial sting out of them. She then returns them to Paul, who absorbs them and is now able to overcome that feeling he had before of being entirely alone, which turned out to be false.

When the emotional lightening bolts have subsided, they return to the playground and Mary goes back to the tactics she has employed up to now in those first six minutes, going through the phases of sadness, desperation, fury and finally of close physical proximity combined with tenderness in order to restore the bond of attachment.

A therapist goes through similar experiences when she is with a patient in the clinic. The clinic is like a laboratory which has the advantage of being able to reproduce many of these emotional elements, most of them remnants of old relationships usually forged in the patient's childhood. These models become projected unconsciously onto the therapist. In order for the therapist to be able to receive them clearly it is vital that the therapist maintain a blank screen. She needs to control her own opinions and prejudices as much as possible. By not mixing her personal experience with that of the patient, she is able to distinguish more clearly what is coming from the patient and what is not, thus improving the analytical experience.

Through a process of trial and error the therapist is able not only to recognize the consequences of the rupture in the chain of attachment but she can also accompany the patient on his journey of exposure without falling into the simplistic trap of taking things personally or reacting to the patient in a defensive way that might reflect feelings of revenge, sadness or even fury. The therapist's weapons like Mary's are those of self-observation, recognition, empathy and containment. Her ability to frame her hypothesis and communicate it freely to the patient should be unhindered by any inclination to take things personally. In this way, the therapist is able to absorb the level of the patient's consciousness.

Through regular clinical practice the therapist is able to accompany the patient along the specific stages of his lonely journey of separation and trauma. More often than not the therapist is doing this somewhat blindly, feeling her way. The patient presents himself at a moment in time that does not actually coincide with the initial manifestation of the pathology. In fact, from the very beginning, the therapist is faced with what appears to be an irreconcilable situation because the patient is already quite advanced in his own strategies for confronting his situation.

So the therapist cannot assume the sequence of events exactly as indicated in the example in the park. She finds himself in a completely new situation with no prior knowledge. She has no historical references, as was the case with Mary or Luisa in relation to little Paul.

In order to dig up clues, a good therapist takes detailed notes of the patient's history as the basis for diagnosis and therapy. However, even the best history-taking has substantial limitations as direct questioning cannot investigate or shed light on everything. This is because the patient himself is confused without realizing it. If he were clear about his situation he would not be suffering. It is this very confusion that has led the patient to seek help.

Very often the therapist has to resort to other strategies in order to try to clarify the emotional elements of the patient's trauma. These are sophisticated strategies that make use of the therapist's own personality in order to seek out the right pathways in an indirect way. They are based on monitoring the feelings the patient transfers to the therapist and sentiments they provoke in the therapist. In other words if they are feelings of rejection or lack of empathy, a working hypothesis would be to localize the trauma in its third stage; if they are of despair, then the second stage would be appropriate and if of desperate anxiety, then the first.

Therapists know that rarely do these phases follow any prescribed order or they can overlap and complicate the situation further. These complications can, on occasion, provide helpful clues towards the prognosis of a patient.

John Bowlby pioneered the description of these stages of separation and the rupture of the links of attachment. Scientific observations indicate that these same phases over time manifest themselves as characteristics embedded in the individual's psyche, converting them into a permanent part of his personality.

People who are particularly flexible and adaptable and who can regain their balance within a reasonable period of time are described as "secure attachments" in order to differentiate them from those classified as "insecure". Similarly, they found that amongst the insecure ones two subtypes could be identified: the "anxious dependants" and the "detached independents". The former demonstrated a greater tendency for proximity with the attachment figure, displaying intense, anxious and fearful signs as if they did not dare leave the folds of their mother's skirts in order to make sure they would not be abandoned. The latter more inclined to "detachment, separation and rejection" maintained an emotional distance in order to avoid the risk of disillusionment.

The traumatic experience of being separated from the attachment figure was recreated in a laboratory for the first time by Mary Ainsworth and her collaborators. In those days they called it "the strange situation". Similar lengths of time for the periods of separation were used. As scientists, they added the presence of an experiment observer between the mother and her son. This type of experiment has been repeated on numerous occasions with certain variations. More recent investigations have placed electrodes on the body and in the brain of the child in order to measure his physiological activity. Parameters as diverse as the response/galvanic resistance of the skin and arterial pressure have been measured. Amongst other things these investigations have demonstrated that in the third phase of cold rejection in which Paul seems to have everything under control the physiological parameters showed that the inner response was as intense as that or the first two phases. This came as a surprise to the protagonist himself who was convinced of his auto control. This explains in part declarations from people who find themselves stuck in this phase of development, one in which they themselves are proud of their own sense of emotional coldness and brittle self-sufficiency which they interpret as a form of security and self-confidence.

Years later, in successive tests they found that there were always a small percentage of children who did not fall unto any of these three categories. This is the case with people whose pasts contain unexpected and extraordinarily traumatic ruptures with their maternal links. These were eventually identified as "disorganized" by researcher Mary Main.

The equivalent within the context of the park would be a bomb going off or the sudden death of the mother. In this hypothetical case Paul would experience emotional chaos, racing towards the nearby bench to look for his mother, realizing that she was gone for good, running away from the next bench in panic and desperation, recognising his need for protection and running back to the bench in search of that security, and so on, in a continuing vicious circle that is difficult to resolve or put a stop to. This mix of emotions occurs so rapidly that it confounds both Paul and any observer. It makes it impossible to follow normal pathways of communication causing frustration and exhaustion in spite of the best of intentions. This confusion leads to the abandonment of any efforts to secure recovery. If this frustration among those who care for Paul is perceived by him, it contributes further to his feeling of disconnection and increases his sense of panic and fury.

This situation is well known in the treatment of complicated cases. They tend to be people with excessively traumatic experiences in childhood. They were witnesses to severe illness in their parents, which left the children functionally if not definitively orphaned, without anything one could begin to describe as parental care. Or they were victims of serious physical, emotional and sexual abuse often perpetrated by the parents themselves or people close to the family. In these cases where the abuse stems from individuals so close to the family, the child's confusion is at its greatest. The trauma is doubled. Firstly because of the transgression of boundaries; secondly and most damagingly because of the betrayal by a person in a position of trust, having to endure threats in order to keep the abuse hidden from others and not being believed by those closest to them when they dared ask for help.

Novice therapists stigmatise these "difficult" patients by attaching pejorative adjectives to them like "manipulators". In order to understand this error one has to be aware of the fact that the patient's disorganized reactions are unconsciously being transferred to the therapist. The therapist becomes stretched to her limits and unable to contain this level of stress, resulting in totally unjustifiably and in an unpleasant manner she projects it back onto the patient.

In actual fact, although it might appear to the contrary, the patient is not a liar, he is simply incapable of describing events in an uninhibited way, fearful of the reprisals he experienced and the dire consequences that followed whenever he tried to tell the truth as a child. There is no original malevolent desire per se to manipulate or attention-seek.

It is to be expected that the observer or therapist may find herself incapable of keeping up with the speed of the patient's traumatic response, remaining trapped within an atmosphere of contagious confusion, lack of clarity and inconsistent communication. This speed of response from the patient can be so disconcerting to the therapist and create a feeling of such acute unease, unpleasantness and discomfort that she can find herself beyond the bounds of tolerance. As she begins to lose her way, instead of maintaining her position as the patient's objective observer, she begins to feel the need to defend herself and slides into primitive methods of projection, handling control over to the patient. This is why it is easy to fall into the trap of erroneously interpreting the patient's demeanour as one that is seeking to provoke and annoy on purpose.

Scientific logic does not support this conclusion. However, the therapist is not only a scientific observer, she is also human. She has her own emotional reactions, her limitations and her mistakes. When these reach a stage of panic they take over from her own independent logic, making her more subject to her own desires than she would wish. Both inexperienced and experienced therapists can go through the same tensions and disturbances when treating patients that are so disturbed.

What is needed is a "subjective focus" in order to be able to identify what represents the transitional projections or transitional objects in the patient's mind. After all, without his subjective perspective we are left with no more than the teddy bear's pieces of cloth, thread, and straw stuffing.

In order to achieve a successful outcome when dealing with the most difficult cases the therapist requires much more than good theoretical training. She needs personal experience as a patient in order to help develop her capacity to mentalise which is based on her own experience of being lost in the depths of the unconscious with the accompanying anxiety and convolutions of therapy. The release of a therapist's compassion is based on the memory of "I have been there too" combined with a special kind of hope that stems from the internal affirmation "if my own therapist stood by me I can now also withstand this period with you". This generational transmission of hope is not different from the example of Mary in the Park. We could assume that Mary would be able to remember at some level, her own positive experience of being held in mind by her own mother perhaps in a different park in her own childhood.

But above all, the therapist requires supervision; no matter how advanced she may consider herself to be. As Carl Jung, the Swiss psychoanalyst mentioned "Even the Pope has a father confessor". Nobody is exempt from making an error. In this knowledge, one can only make plans and allow oneself time to reflect. One needs somebody else in order to guard against forgetfulness or self-deception. An experienced supervisor is someone who knows the therapist, can identify when the therapist has lost her way and can help recalibrate her personal and professional objectivity.

In conclusion…

The adventure of psychotherapy is a relationship that reproduces many of a child's most basic and vital connections with his principal attachment figures, like his mother. On the one hand the adventure is helped along by a natural desire to find proximity and protection and on the other by exploration of the unknown.

Curiosity leads to separation from familiar physical and mental landmarks that, in their time, represented security. The relationship is a dynamic one and involves a shifting forwards and backwards together with daring to confront ever increasing levels if risk. This attachment figure is not limited to the traditional figure of the mother; it also extends to many other significant people in the course of a lifetime.

These processes, which are in principle external, gradually become internalized and make up part of the most intimate auto-images linked to our identity and self-esteem.

In a certain way this dependence is never completely overcome. The nineteenth and early twentieth century myth of psychological growth from dependence to social independence became gradually substituted by the impact of the theory of attachment. The concept of gradual progress from immaturity to mature interdependence was found to be more convincing. In addition the myth of being able to obtain a concrete psychological position with an iron-cast division between our external conduct and the interior workings of the mind changed with the proposition of the theory of transitional space and objects. This is a more malleable concept, far from functional determinism, perhaps in line with what appears to be a better understanding of the functioning of the brain according to modern physiology and its concept of plasticity.

It is the territory of the "as if.…", of imagination, and play, that offers true meaning.

As with good parenting, success of patient-therapist relations is not strictly based on the absence or reduction of problems, rather on an emerging resilience. This is based on the ability to reconnect and repair most setbacks.

What is fascinating about the story of Mary and Paul is the humble recognition that the majority of models built around our human relationships stem from the cradle of infancy, in maternal nurturing and simple animal instincts both alternative and complementary surrounding areas of security and of exploration.

Chapter 5

✳ ✳ ✳

IS THE PATIENT
MOTIVATED?

Now that a number of years have gone by I can revisit and welcome the memories I hold of my initiation into psychiatry. One of my very first patients suffered from alcohol dependence. After an hour of evaluation and diagnosis I proposed a plan of action for him which, to my surprise, although he accepted it gratefully he never managed to follow. The conclusion, shared by my colleagues, was that the patient was not sufficiently motivated.

He came back several times looking for help. I often felt frustrated by his resistance. All I could do was suggest he come back when he felt motivated. I had put a great deal of effort and dedication into his case after recommending that he be admitted to the ward for detoxification. He had come to appreciate my efforts but they made him feel guilty. Partly because of this, he left feeling ashamed, asking my forgiveness and was convinced he had failed me.

It was the research and publications of Prochaska and Di Clemente in the 1970s that changed the perspective of motivation in the treatment of addiction and later, by extrapolation, of many other areas of psychopathology. They analysed the concept of motivation from research studies into ten thousand smokers. They focused not so much on diagnosis and evaluation of the severity of the illness but rather on analysing what was actually happening in clinical practice. Their results challenged the prevailing views. The concept of motivation became something more dynamic and complex than the ideas that had been taken on face value until then.

This new point of view did not lie in simply considering whether the patient was motivated enough to begin therapy. It was principally based on the presumption that motivation is always present. The researchers discovered that motivation can be recognized in one form or another even when it is latent. Consequently the focus of clinical exploration becomes one that seeks to find out what stage of motivation the individual has reached in relation to that particular problem and that particular stage in his or her life.

Prochaska and Di Clemente evolved a circular pattern of behaviour. This cycle of motivation was divided into five distinctly defined phases. They are pre-contemplation, contemplation, action, maintenance and relapse. They also reached the conclusion that different therapeutic interventions could be classified and matched to suit any particular phase appropriately and effectively.

Thus when a smoker finds himself in the pre-contemplative phase, that is one where he does not consider smoking to be a hazard, what he most needs is information. In the next phase, the contemplative phase, the smoker decides to explore the advantages and disadvantages of smoking in relation to his own health. Once his interest has been awakened and armed with more comprehensive information, he can weigh up the advantages and disadvantages of carrying on smoking or giving it up.

The next stage is one where the patient makes a decision to take action. This decision can be positive, for example the decision to follow a specific treatment or negative, to go on as before. If the decision to take action is sufficiently firm, it is only in that critical moment that the clinician's task of setting out the different treatment options will make sense to the patient.

Once one of these methods has been chosen there is a greater chance of success at the end of the treatment. Assuming that this phase is complete one can move on to the next phase, that of keeping up the new behaviour. At this point the amount of clinical intervention is doubled. It helps to overcome this temporary period of temptation to return to past habits and re-enforces a positive attitude.

If, for whatever reason, the smoker should have a relapse, the atmosphere of success is dramatically replaced by one of failure and denial. Failure and denial go together with escaping the seriousness of the habit, a return to a pre-contemplative phase. This new phase of pre-contemplation is often dominated by a conscious avoidance of the matter in order not to revive the pain and low self-esteem brought on by the previous relapse. The appropriate reaction requires a different tone, involving a certain amount of understanding in order to counter the feelings of catastrophe and of guilt. This ability to listen and to display a certain tolerance helps with the necessary period of waiting for the recovery of strength and for the return of the will to continue. This marks the end of the period of pre-contemplation taking us back once again to the beginning of the active motivation cycle.

In their investigations Prochaska and Di Clemente found that the phenomenon of relapse occurred quite frequently and that it occurred, on average, four times before a successful outcome showing a substantial change in behaviour was achieved.

In the practice of psychotherapy we find that the treatment of personal problems has a similar approach to that of the treatment of addictions in the sense that it also includes cycles of motivation and the need for repetition. In some ways one could also describe these personal problems as having certain characteristics of addiction. Quite often slow progress or failure does not depend solely on the skill and tactics of the therapist. My experience with the patient with alcohol problems is a good example. In this case my insistence on applying certain direct action techniques when the patient was in the very earliest stages of motivation was premature. The patient was simply not ready. My own interpretation at the time, that the patient was not sufficiently motivated, was not correct. Now that time has passed I have come to realise that as a therapist I was not experienced enough to be able to distinguish between the different stages of engagement and I committed a serious error.

When practicing psychotherapy this "timing" or ability to intervene at the right moment is highly relevant. This opportune moment is often shrouded with subtlety and hidden behind the variety of masks used in the presentation of problems.

Let us look, for example, at the case of a patient who is seeking help to resolve problems he has had with a relative. The therapist should avoid the mistake of focusing on solutions before she has a clear idea not only of the cause or causes of the problem but more importantly of the patient's stage of receptivity and of the emotional availability he has at his disposal in order to confront his problems. The therapist knows that the process the patient has gone through in order to reach this particular stage should not be underestimated. On the contrary, confidence and the key to a good relationship rest on seizing the right opportunity. She knows that, as with the smokers, she has to attempt the same process, or variations of it, over and over again making use of any temporary setbacks as a platform of knowledge and adjustment in preparation for the next attempt, until success is obtained.

The situation becomes even more complex when the patient initially presents with multiple problems and when each one is at a different stage of motivation. In this case therapy can be used in an attempt to resolve the problems in the order in which they are presented, one at a time. It is more common, especially in the case of more dynamic and interpersonal therapies, for these problems to interact to the point where dealing with them one by one is not possible. One example could be a patient presenting with a mixture of alcohol dependence, combined with marital conflict, and a crisis at work. In this case the therapist tackles the three conflicts at the same time but selects different strategies for each one, depending on the patient's stage of motivation towards each particular subject, without losing sight of the picture as a whole. It is possible for the patient to be at the pre-contemplation stage in relation to alcohol, that is to say that he may not even be aware that this was relevant to his situation. He could, at the same time, be at the action stage with regard to his marital situation whilst he could be in the relapse stage of his work problems.

In reality what the therapist does is to behave like a gardener in an allotment. He knows when to plant and when to gather the fruits. He understands that there is a time for everything, like picking tomatoes in spring, strawberries in summer, grapes in autumn and oranges in winter. And in each particular case he knows how patiently to share out the tasks in his garden, preparing the earth, selecting the seeds, sewing the seeds whilst fertilizing others, harvesting in time before a storm, pruning, knowing how to wait and apply his skills at just the right time on order to get the best results.

The seasoned gardener has learned that each one of these phases has its own peculiarities. Although his knowledge of the cycles of nature acts as a guide, experience tells him that he must remain open to the vagaries of each moment, feeling his way towards the next step. He knows that where science ends, art begins and he takes full advantage of the integration of both of these facets.

The therapist in the clinic not only differentiates between the different stages of motivation but just like the gardener sets to work on them. The therapist needs to know how to prepare the terrain, when to begin to outline dilemmas, how to nurture them, how to make careful investigations by gathering more information, how to respect the need for rest and assimilation, when to separate and put the pressure on, a bit like a greenhouse works, when to prune away unnecessary branches and when to put on the finishing touches in order to pick the fruits before they become overripe.

All of this points not to a business with concrete, mechanical objectives but rather to an art form, based on experience and the knowledge of universal models of relationships, their timing and their requirements; an art form that is open to unforeseen surprises and setbacks and open in a dynamic way to the necessities and creative opportunities offered by each unique.

Chapter 6

* * *

SHERLOCK HOLMES

One of the strategies employed by Sherlock Holmes, the hero of Sir Arthur Conan Doyle's famous novels, is to return to the scene of the crime in order to identify and eventually ensnare the criminal.

The idea is that, in order to complete the investigation, the detective should cast a sharp eye around the crime scene knowing that the criminal always feels compelled to return to the scene of the crime. This is the method adopted in the novels in order to uncover conclusive evidence about the suspect and speed up the solution to the case.

The question is why does the criminal return to the scene of the crime?

The most logical explanation is perhaps because the criminal is unsure in his own mind as to his/her ability to control every detail of the event. Consequently, the criminal attempts to reconstruct the scene, visualising every step, trying to find the pieces of the puzzle that are missing and dwelling obsessively on the failures that led him to lose control and perform the final act of violence.

This metaphor can be applied to some psychotherapeutic strategies and to their ultimate resolution. In psychotherapy the return is to the original trauma.

For some reason the symptoms of this trauma that occurred in the past, acquire their own autonomy and, after a while, cease to be associated with their original cause.

If we are able to overcome certain memory blocks, the origin of the symptoms under psychological investigation, can take us to the very instant when the patient became traumatised; the moment when he could not contain, manage or direct the situation he found himself in.

The failure to properly integrate memories carries with it a sense of incompleteness that repeatedly resurfaces. Psychotherapists analyse these patterns and draw up theories about the mental processes involved, which follow along very similar lines to those of a detective inquiry. For example, by not confronting the original conflict, the consequent pain and anxiety can exceed the bounds of tolerance. The patient's mind develops symptoms which he tries to play down, ignoring the growing discomfort and intensity of feeling, at the same time developing ever more cunning and ultimately costly defence mechanisms.

In practice the investigator traces events from front to back.

Days, weeks, months and even years later this incomplete trauma can go round and round in the patient's head, or can linger in the unconscious, creating a swelling dissonance.

The therapist, in conversation during clinical sessions, is like a policewoman checking her beat in a patrol car. If she suddenly finds something unusual or suspicious, she slows down in order to get a better look. It's part of her job – to observe and pick up information discreetly from a distance- so as not to alert the suspect.

But sometimes it is necessary to stop – to get out of the car and approach the scene quietly and confidently in order to make a closer inspection – to ask questions in the vicinity – even to question the suspect himself, probing for information, attempting to provoke a personal reaction or an evasive answer that might give the policewoman a lead. She might even try to increase the suspect's nervousness and anxiety with intentionally casual remarks like "We shall see", "if I were you I'd be very careful", "I'll be back tomorrow to do another round", then get back in the car set off on her rounds again.

Quite often when setting out on a psychotherapeutic exploration, the therapist begins with peripheral symptoms, seemingly disconnected, that appears absurd when linked with the apparent circumstances surrounding the current situation. But after a short while persistence, curiosity and clinical examination increasingly reveal new evidence.

To a certain extent the investigative technique is like doing a puzzle. First you gather together pieces with similar colours and themes. Then you line the edge bits up then you fill up a whole corner, moving from the easiest to the most difficult and sometimes simultaneously between the two.

It is all very much, as Freud indicated, like an arqueological dig into the past. Revealing the unconscious layer by layer brings one closer to what can be described as the hypothetical yawn from the earliest chapters of the patient's very personal and particular history, helping reconstruct early behaviour and allowing the therapist to travel with increasing confidence towards the nub of the matter.

This reconstruction is based not only on memories of words and behaviour but more subtly on memories of thoughts and emotions that have had a profound and intimate influence on the person's belief that he is the protagonist. It is these shades of emotional and personal cognition that contribute to a patient sense of wholeness. This is when the long-forgotten and ignored pieces of the puzzle that did not fit together, find their place and meaning, making it possible to interconnect all the evidence and thus create a cohesive and relevant narrative history.

Sometimes, given the passage of time, the memory can only find remnants of memories. Then the only recourse is to allow the imagination free reign combining this with past experience of similar cases in order to arrive at an approximate reconstruction. So the detective-therapist needs to exercise all her powers of observation and memory, patiently gathering clues, similarities, differences, and returning to the case over and over again from another angle. Making use of her imagination and association of ideas, she develops theories and hypotheses which she tests against the growing body of evidence.

This creative process is more circular than linear. It needs to be based on a capacity for abstraction, without allowing the concrete elements of reality to take over. It is rather like putting on a pair of shoes belonging to the patient and very slowly taking steps forward in them. At other times it is like travelling down several different avenues at the same time trying to fish for hidden and often forgotten events.

In this case the therapist is no different from a fisherman, who puts the right bait on the hook, waits for the fish to bite, eases the rod and line little by little, avoids using undue force might risk snapping the line and ruining the result, knowing that in time the fish will tire.

The therapist well knows that her prey is often trapped in the past, and that it can be persuaded to come to the surface attracted by pain as the bait even though its habitat is still in the depth of the sea of the unconscious, deep down in a dense dark world of the hidden and forgotten. Aware that these oceanic depths have their cycles, their tides and their currents, the therapist knows that if they are minutely observed and shown the respect they deserve, they will eventually become more amenable.

So it is that, little by little, at last the ultimate liberation of the mind can take place, a mind that has long been held captive by a colossal nightmare.

It is only when the story has been exhaustively investigated, with all its emotional implications that the mind is ready to leave it behind and relegate it to the archives of history. Only then can the story remain archived as a case that has been successfully solved and closed.

The dynamics of the puzzle of the liberation of the unconscious is a mystery. Unlike the detective or the fisherman, that strive to catch the allusive prey, the patient's mind becomes the therapist main ally and collaborates with the therapists in its ultimate release.

Chapter 7

THE ARMY

E ntering into group therapy is an adventure, a bit like getting into training for the army. After some initial tests screening for motivation and ability the candidate is informed as to what lies ahead.

The decision to join up is entirely voluntary. But once you are in, the group has its rules, boundaries and code of conduct. The first thing a conscript has to do is attend training camp. The purpose of this phase is to provide the soldier with the physical and psychological skills he will need in order to operate more competently in the theatre of war.

War is dangerous. People get wounded and die as a consequence. The purpose of the training camp is to maximise the soldier's skills through discipline, exposure to fear and a host of other obstacles and difficulties. In this way he not only acquires strength and the ability to adapt both physically and mentally to the current circumstances, but he also learns ways of interacting with his team and working together in order to survive in combat.

The training regime does not allow the soldier to choose to get up in the morning whenever he likes, or to reflect and make individual decisions according to his own particular taste or fancy. For example, should a soldier choose not to throw himself to the ground because he wants to keep his outfit clean and pressed, or should he (or she) decide to eat à la carte and duck out_of the afternoon gym session preferring to have a nap instead, one would doubt this soldier's ability to succeed in his task.

Training means exposing an individual to a specific, gradual and consistent series of challenges at every level, often reaching the very limits of normal human tolerance, in order to develop resistance, flexibility, calm, and fast reactions not only under normal circumstances but also in extreme circumstances where primitive survival instincts like fear and terror predominate and where inconsistencies abound.

Traditionally this type of training is conducted by the sergeant major. He is usually portrayed as harsh, dry, and demanding with little time for personal niceties. In this context soldiers go through various phases where, once confronted with this strong disciplinarian, they begin to feel resentment towards this authority figure who holds the power to impose sanctions, limit their behaviour and ultimately decide whether the soldier will make the grade or not.

The need to learn how to work together as a team accounts for a large part of the more exacting nature of the training. Building up a working relationship with the other soldiers is not easy. Fellow soldiers do not always turn out to be ideal workmates. Personality clashes arise together with problems of reciprocity, different backgrounds, cultures and levels of intelligence. Fear causes these problems to become intensified, acquiring a greater significance than they would in ordinary relationships in peacetime. Differences in the way conscripts react under stress exacerbate the prevailing atmosphere of tension and conflict. The pain of being away from a previous family environment, fear, expectation, selfishness and idiosyncratic conflicts make this enforced cohabitation at close quarters an enormous challenge for all concerned. But by the same token these very difficulties in themselves can offer up opportunities - opportunities in the midst of danger and panic - to learn and develop qualities like the capacity to keep thinking and holding onto responsibility for themselves and for the group, qualities of short term sacrifice in the interest of long term gains, of sacrifice for the greater good, opportunities to gain perspective, efficiency, an improved demeanour, respect for procedure, hierarchical command and diplomacy.

Group therapy is not like shaping an army but there are similarities in the training procedure. These similarities arise from the interaction between a group of people who have never met before and who come together with the common purpose of trying to understand themselves a little better and of learning to interact with others.

Just as the soldier's training involves the specialised knowledge and the wise use of weapons, so the patient in a psychotherapy group learns to develop and use a special form of reciprocal emotional literacy that targets his needs and those of others. In fact the whole group develops a common language based on an unfolding history of shared images and experiences.

Members of a therapy group recognise they cannot achieve all of this by themselves so they seek out a guide and the opportunity to work together as a group. They understand that unity means strength. They share a wish to learn from past errors, to change bad habits into more acceptable behaviour and to dare to rehearse them live in front of the group whilst at the same maintaining a common contract of strict confidentiality in order to create an atmosphere of trust and continuing progress thus avoiding any unnecessary humiliation.

The group has a set of rules and regulations that provide a certain sense of security. It also has the therapist, or several therapists, whose job it is to keep the long term goals in mind, to devise ways of achieving them, to reflect on the developing situation, to be self-reliant and by means of a pre-determined style and approach to be able to raise the group's morale when necessary.

People who join group therapy are needy, having often had conflicts and suffered trauma when forming relationships not just with others or members of the family but with themselves. It is as though they are in the midst of a battle between inter and intra personal relationships and the battleground is the social arena.

Signing up for this type of training offers the promise of an atmosphere where one can develop qualities like flexibility, the ability to adapt, better understanding, reflection, insight and the chance to acquire new skills for life. The training allows the participants to enter into live role-playing and to make mistakes without doing any damage, as happens in a normal social context. For example, trying to impose a more assertive stance with a family member at an inappropriate time can have dire consequences that will be remembered for the rest of the participant's life.

Therapy is not a Shangri-La, like the famous place described by James Hilton in his book, later made into a film. high up in the Himalayas, Shangri-La was a place where peace and harmony was maintained through a spiritual master and where time stood still. On the contrary, although therapy requires a certain level of idealisation, it is not a utopia where one is always understood, accepted and admired, where the therapist knows exactly what to do and never makes a mistake. This is an excessively idealised fantasy though in itself forms part of the necessary therapeutic process. Both in Shangri-La and in the unconscious the passing of time has no effect unless the boundaries of isolation are crossed.

When this idealisation is analysed for what it is, it reveals an avoidance of the starkness of reality. The group, rather like a mini laboratory, a microcosm of reality, carries with it life's difficulties, its challenges, the need to learn patience, tolerance and an acceptance of one's personal limitations and those of others and of society as a whole. It means re-visiting, in the flesh over and over again any unbalanced reactions that have stemmed from distorted ideas and misunderstandings. These initial awkward and often ugly reactions are inevitable in this lengthy educational process. As in every educational setting, repetition is required until the objective begins to define itself in a more elegant, acceptable and useful shape. This repetition, gradual and unexpected as it may be, cannot rid the participant of the awkwardness of his first efforts, and the passing hurt and rejection involved, despite his initial sense of pride as a creative entrepreneurial contributor.

In addition, the projection onto the therapist of personal inadequacies and frustrations is not unlike the hate soldiers feel towards the figure of sergeant major. These projections are also part of the initial stage of the experience when the therapist is perceived as an authority figure, and the source of a curtailed freedom, a cruel figure, strict, persecuting, retaliatory and ultimately uncompromising.

It is not the therapist's job to destroy the fantasies that unfold before her but rather, through her silence, to encourage their imaginative development within the safe confines of the therapeutic contract. She knows that a half-hearted approach would never have the same effect in spite of the great temptation to avoid creating tension by engaging in explanatory techniques, or indulging in vindictiveness or neglect. The tactful resistance, on the part of the therapist, not to destroy the unfolding fantasies serves to avoid the consequences of uncontrolled fears in the patient originating from childhood experiences with his or her parents.

The good therapist does not reveal her secrets. Just like a magician or illusionist the therapist strives to maintain the illusion to the very end. She knows that any impulse from the patient to attack or destroy her would recreate the fury felt by the patient against the authority figures of his childhood. The therapist prefers to focus on and facilitate the projection of repressed fantasies just as the magician's act displays swords piercing the body, bodies being set alight, being chopped into little pieces and sometimes vanishing altogether. The patient, like the spectator of the magician's act unconsciously collaborates in this violent and destructive scenario as if he were attempting to rid himself of the monster he senses within.

Then the magician vanishes. His assistant searches in vain here there and everywhere. The audience is left in a state of suspense.

Very soon a sense of sorrow and guilt creeps in.

Then, to everyone's surprise and delight, the magician reappears. The spectator feels instant relief at the fact that the magician has been restored to life very much like the relief felt by the patient when he realises that the therapist has survived the blind and unleashed forces of his (the patient's) unconscious. The therapist has proved that these forces are, after all, part of life and do not need to be hidden in the prison of internal secrets.

The patient, like the spectator of a magician's act, passes from the emotional challenge on to another phase of reawakened curiosity and enquiry. He begins to ask himself, "What happened? How does he do it? What is the trick?"

Once he realises that these feelings are not as dangerous as he had thought, the patient sets free his impulse for exploration and says to himself "If he can do it, why not I?" The patient passes from the role of passive spectator to one where he takes the initiative. He dares to try to do the same and thus regains his role as protagonist. This transition from a passive to an active role brings with it a new perspective rebuilds.

The patient becomes aware of the negative aspect that he has been projecting onto therapist. His compulsive need, therefore, to target the therapist diminishes and with it his dependence on her. This dependence was not only upon her as the recipient of his previously disowned unpleasant feelings but also as the magical rescuer from his alienation. Painfully the patient realises that the therapist is not an extension of himself that he can control at will. This leads him to conclude that he must inevitably rely on his own personal efforts to seek feedback from other members of his group resulting in a greater ability to discriminate better between expectations and achievable aims. By working together both individuals and the group as a whole regain their own sense of authority.

The group, as a mini-laboratory of reality, carries with it its own problems, its challenges, the need to display patience, tolerance, acceptance of one's own limitations, the limitations of others and of society itself. Any imbalance that arise from concepts that are erroneous or poorly understood can, only when felt in the flesh, result in a realisation of the advantages of interdependence. The group is constantly learning how to negotiate a dynamic distance between its members that will allow collaboration and creativity without losing its sense of individual identity. As in all educational situations, many ways of testing the situation are required, with seemingly endless repetition until the objective begins to emerge in a more agreeable, complete, acceptable and useful way.

Eventually, the time comes for the conscripts at the training camp to pass out, say goodbye to their friends and prepare themselves for the next stage, very often a period of action on the front line. One part of them feels sad and insecure about leaving the training camp. Another part feels unhappy, convinced that there will never be a perfect ending. This sense of mature dissatisfaction provides the fuel essential to the further exploration of life. They have learned that their training will continue for the rest of their lives and that what took place in the first few months at the training camp was enough just to be able to move ahead.

In the final phases of a healthy psychotherapeutic group, the patients learn to detach themselves from the exclusivity of the group setting and to realise that the application of their progress in terms of authority and intimacy needs to be put to the test in real life. Sometimes they forget that their desire to relate better to people in to real life was the reason why they joined the group in the first place, preferring to prolong their therapy unnecessarily. It is then that they learn how to make their farewells consciously, in an attempt perhaps to put right so many clumsy farewells of the past. Learning how to end things is just as important as knowing how to begin things.

In this final phase, very much like the soldier who takes away with him his memories of the sergeant major, the patient always carries with him his memories of the therapist. Often they are silently evoked like invisible helpers when faced with life's big decisions. In fact, some of the effects of the group may surprise the patient after a considerable period of time.

Not unlike veteran soldiers, once their term of service is over, perhaps meeting over a coffee to reminisce about old times at the army training camp, they will jokingly conjure up the figure of the benign sergeant major. It is only much later that the patient may come to realise the importance of this firm and challenging figure. It is then that he discovers the connection between his frustration at imposed therapeutic boundaries and the underlying motives of tough love.

Chapter 8

✳ ✳ ✳

COMPUTER ANTI-VIRUS

When the brain is overwhelmed (becomes saturated) with stimuli, especially emotional stimuli, it sets up defence mechanisms. In an attempt to describe how this functions, I shall explore certain links with other defence mechanisms both physical, as in the human body, and technical as in computer systems.

The organizing capacities of the human mind, the immune system and computers all have similarities in the way they process memory. The entering and storage of data and the speed with which it is processed affects the working of the rest of the system. Memory has an intrinsic and uniquely innate capacity to expand itself with each successive input as in the process of computer downloading and different learning processes in human behaviour.

This organizing capacity can become diminished, either because of birth defects, injury or conflict. It may be that some of the system's components are faulty. Sometimes these can be repaired or substituted. Alternatively the operative systems can clash as a result of external interference if all measures of protection, repair and maintenance fail to counteract the invasion.

This is what viruses can do.

It is curious that the self-same word "virus" is used in computer technology just as it is in the field of biology. A viral attack blocks or harms certain functions, some more apparent than others. Sometimes one only becomes aware of the damage when it is too late to put it right. Experience tells us that these attacks to the system are not isolated cases, but a daily phenomenon.

As such, computers just as the human body have evolved over time ever more complex defence mechanisms. Human beings are subject to a vast rhythm of sensory, intellectual and emotional information. We also have a psychological defence mechanism. This constant bombardment of information in daily life, in terms of quantity as much as quality, can sometimes be too much to cope with and consequently becomes toxic to the system.

This differs from the way the immune system works on that this toxicity is not based on a physical entity that can be detected and isolated with a microscope. This external toxic assault on the mind as well as on the computer system is a flow of electro-chemical activity that is received and transmitted through the system by neurons and conductors.

Although this offensive attack is not actually tangible, it requires a solid base like a computer or the human body itself in order to be able to set its activities in motion, the consequences of which are not simply alterations in magnetic or electrochemical conduction, but sometimes actual physical harm.

Defence mechanisms activate the anti-virus programme, firstly in order to evaluate the situation and then, if possible, to cancel the fault and at a later stage repair the damage and its effects or if this were not possible to eliminate or encapsulate the fault from the entire system. All of this requires energy and chunks of memory which need to be drawn from available supplies. This involves certain temporary adjustments which affect the speed of the computer and the body and mind's ability to function properly. Once the problem has been solved the need to focus so much energy on defence mechanisms diminishes thus freeing up the memory capacity. The original speed is re-established allowing the computer, the body or the mind to function efficiently once again. Using the example of the computer, when there is a major breakdown, the computer becomes sluggish – it freezes, stops responding to commands or it reacts catastrophically and behaves in a way that could be described as "electronic delirium".

If we draw a parallel with the immune system and take as an example a specific event like a blow to the body, the response involves swelling, a heating up and reddening of the skin, acute sensitivity to the mildest touch which in turn alerts the body to the need to protect that area from external danger. This phase allows the body time to focus on that particular point and allow its full defence potential to flourish. The next phase is when temporary scar tissue forms which protects the surface area enabling the deeper tissue to regenerate and become more resilient.

If, by any ill luck an infection should develop and spread through the whole body, the normal functioning of the body would slow down, generating signs of tiredness that lead to the need for rest and withdrawal in order to facilitate the immunological response. Often fever will occur and the basic functions of the body will be affected, like appetite, sleep and general alertness. In extreme cases these symptoms will lead to a state of delirium and loss of consciousness.

When a psychological event takes place, like trauma, conflict, or a lack of basic information, these cause maladjustment in the mind and set off a defence mechanism. The mind seeks to separate the wheat from the chaff and sifts out any elements that may be unnecessary or counterproductive. Energy is required for this, psychic energy as well as physical energy. Consciousness begins to slow down; the ability to take in new information seems to become limited and in serious cases closes down altogether. Then a form of emotional fever can set in, a general heating up, when the individual becomes hypersensitive to external stimuli and culminating in emotional delirium or stupor. These states are commonly described as being "out of mind" and are an expression of the limitations of psychological containment. The system defaults to the simplest and most basic mode when the mind is not capable of abstractions or hypothetical conjecture nor a game of fantasy neither does it have time to linger on leisurely reflection.

In spite of its drawbacks this period when defence mechanisms are called up is a necessary one. It is sometimes misunderstood by friends and family who, in an attempt to be helpful, become witness to bad tempered reactions, negativity, and hypersensitivity, reactions which are an unconscious attempt to minimise interference and preserve isolation. I am referring to reactions which often, and perhaps erroneously, are described as narcissistic.

Some time back, in the first half of the 20th Century, the practice of psychoanalysis indicated that narcissism could not easily be treated and it became stigmatised with a poor prognosis. Today we can see that if these bouts of bad humour became worse it was principally because of the underdevelopment of psychoanalysis at that time.

This phenomenon is not very different from the worsening of successive infections of a haematoma if the doctor insists on probing into the wound in spite of the patient's cries of pain. A more appropriate course of action might be that once the surface of the wound is clean, to allow the wound to take its own course and eventually heal itself. Simple things could work like putting a bandage over the wound instead of interfering with it.

By comparison, we need to understand that in the case of psychological wounds, unnecessary probing is not always a better approach than having the confidence to allow the silent repair mechanism of the unconscious mind to do its job.

Psychological defence mechanisms, as with everything in nature, are many and varied and appear to be organized in an ordered, hierarchical fashion in accordance with seriousness of the requirements. At first only the simplest mechanisms are brought into play and then, only if these are not sufficient, are more sophisticated defence mechanism called upon, leaving the most dramatic for the most powerful cases. There is also a certain order in the amount of energy required since the early interventions are less taxing.

Clinical observation in psychiatric practice examines the types of defences that are displayed. In this way clinical observation reveals further clues to the gravity of the situation and the prognosis. As the patient's condition worsens he loses his ability to call upon healthy defences like a sense of humour and opts for more neurotic lines of defence like repression, he may resort to more immature and primitive defences reaching extreme psychotic behaviour.

By psychotic one understands episodes when conscious contact with reality is lost leading to extreme forms of isolation and protection almost like a self-imposed military curfew that allows the mind to survive a state of emergency.

As the patient's recovery advances his defences become aligned with his ever-increasing ability to tolerate reality leading to improved 'attention' and increased in disposable working memory. This allows him to resolve his problems with greater ease, consequently calming down the systems overload he had accumulated before.

When, firstly, certain life circumstances exceed the mind's capacity threshold and then secondly, overwhelm the body's defence mechanism, the patient's unconscious alerts us by creating catastrophic emergency reactions often accompanied by a terror of having too much to do and a loss of control and of the ability to be self-sufficient. This sometimes requires hospital admission, seclusion in a room for longer than is the social norm and/or appropriate pharmacological sedation. In this phase, any attempt at facilitating the expression of pain through explorative therapies that try to dig out the problems runs the risk of re-traumatising the patient.

In these crisis phases many people resort to self - medication and the inappropriate use of alcohol and drugs. This desire to find relief is understandable but as a strategy it is poorly effective in the short term as it simply harms the body with toxic substances. Cleaning out and detoxifying the brain not only has to do with psychological residues, it also has to do with physiochemical and hormonal changes that are directly linked with stress. The re-establishment of balance is achieved principally during rest and more so during sleep.

In order to explain the principle behind this process I am going to use, as an example, the night cleaning services in an office block.

This is an almost anonymous service as it goes on after the conclusion of the day's activities. If, for whatever reason, there should have been an overload of work in the offices and some staff needed to work late, the cleaning staff would not be able to do their work properly and the dirt would accumulate day by day. The cleaners would complain and if the company director decided to try to placate the cleaners' frustration with an easy solution, for example allowing them to drink alcohol during their working nights, he might succeed in making them temporally less aggressive, but as time went on they would insist on more alcohol leading to indescribable chaos. To silence the alarm system would only increase their inefficiency, they would do a bad job, resulting in a progressive accumulation of dirt and rubbish.

In an emergency situation like this, should the company director wish to confront the situation, he would need to analyse the cause of the problem and assess whether or not it stems from an actual conflict or some deficit. An example of conflict is a personal disagreement. An example of deficit is when a cleaning team is inefficient through lack of training. In cases of conflict, interventions that aim to resolve friction are appropriate. In the case of deficits, it would be necessary to plug up the holes with new information, training, new machinery or more personnel.

In the field of mental health there is often room for solutions such as these. For example, the regenerative value of sleep can be liberated by using natural means that don't involve toxic substances like alcohol and drugs. Sometimes pharmacological and psychological interventions can be helpful.

Psychotherapy sets out to discover, analyse the focus of the deficits and/or conflicts and apply solutions that facilitate the unfolding of intrinsic methods of defence that regulate the balanced functioning of the mind.

The way the human mind works is not exactly like the workings of a computer or of the immune system. However, all three are based on a system of articulated connections with their related effects which can offer clues as to the way they function. The more overloaded they are the less efficient they become and the more they need to be cleared out in order to restore normal function.

The emotional significance of experience adds a deeper dimension. The comparison of information technology, the immune system and the human mind can be useful but does not fully encompass the subject. One of the main differences lies in the meaning of emotional experience and its resonance at the psychological and social level which adds a powerful and unpredictable complexity.

Chapter 9

* * *

THE CHAIR WITH MANY LEGS

Allow me to take you by the hand into the following scenario. Firstly, I would like you to imagine a chair you are going to sit on - in this case one-legged chair like a bar stool in a cafeteria. Imagine yourself sitting comfortably on the stool. Then think of what could happen if the stool's leg broke while you were sitting on it. It would almost certainly fall to the ground taking you with it.

Now what if the chair was different and had two or three legs and again, after a while, one of the legs broke? The same thing would happen; the chair would collapse to the ground. And if the chair had four legs and one of them broke? You would immediately notice that it had become unstable. You might lose your balance and tilt over a bit but you would have enough time to regain your balance and avoid a fall. But if we chose to cut another leg off (leaving two) you would still fall down however hard you tried to avoid it.

Some office chairs have five legs, often with wheels on them to enable them to slide around more easily. If one of these legs to fail there need not be a problem. If two of them failed, depending on the position of these two, you might still be able to keep your balance. This could also depend on how alert you were at the time and how aware of your surroundings. But if three or more legs should fail, the fall would be inevitable.

Now imagine a chair that is even more stable, with ten legs for example. You might say this chair was strong and robust enough to be accident proof. If one leg were to break or two or three or four or if even seven legs broke, the chair would still remain standing. But if, by a stroke of ill luck one more leg broke (leaving only two) then, in spite of its original sturdiness, the chair's collapse would be inevitable just as in the previous examples.

Thus, it is evident that the more legs a chair has the more stable it is, however its long term stability cannot be guaranteed, even when all possible risks have been eliminated.

Now please allow me to apply this principle in the context of one's emotional life. Let us look at some parallels.

I should like to emphasize the importance of the convergence of various different sources of support in order to maintain a healthy mental state. These sources of help, illustrated in the previous metaphor through the chair legs, represent different aspects of one's personal life - physical well-being, internal emotional resources like self-worth, resilience, a positive attitude, and personal faith; or external sources of support like work, hobbies, sport, education, family ties, and friends and neighbours. Also important is interaction in your locality, like daily contact with your shopkeepers – the baker, newsagent, tobacconist, café waiter – all of these provide significant support networks in one's external life. There are other more artificial but no less important sources of support, like health and social services. All of this creates a social network that balances out social and emotional isolation.

This network is a dynamic one that reflects the laws of nature. One of these is that everything changes. Nothing is permanently stable in life. Even the most robust health can be toppled by an unexpected viral infection, or by and accident or simply by old age. Any amount of professional preparation can quickly become outdated by the speed of progress. Employment contracts and jobs can be terminated owing to a crisis in the economy. Changes in the market economy and corruption can cause the stock market to crash and savings to disappear. Personal relationships, especially marital ones have never been free of challenging periods, in spite of mutual economic interests and the best of intentions from both sides of the relationship to maintain a permanent commitment. Very old friendships that appeared eternal can vanish from night to morning with no explanation. History has always recorded changes over periods of time in language, culture, tradition, feelings of belonging to a particular community, nationalism and political convictions. Some of these changes may take place several times within a person's lifetime. Even faith held in different religious beliefs has also been known to waver when confronted by unexpected events and the weariness of erosion over a long passage of time.

Given the temporary nature of any source of support, it is natural that we should explore strategies that would overcome the effects of change. One of the tried and tested strategies is to employ a long-term perspective and trust in a combination of these "support-sources". By keeping a close watch in the short term over any deterioration of those very sources of support, appropriate and timely adjustments can be made that will avoid any unexpected surprises in the long term.

Firstly, we should prepare a network of as many sources of support as possible keeping a constant watch for any changes that might occur. As in all states of plenty, its quantity and formation are components of growth.

Secondly, a good investment is required that reinforces the existing legs.

Thirdly, each leg should be checked for quality and practicability and these judgments should be devoid of any romantic or idealistic notions as to their capabilities. For example, maybe under some hypnotic idealistic suggestion we might reject a close friend or companion because he or she is not quite perfect. But a friend, however imperfect, is better than none. Using the example of the chair, a chair leg may not be made of steel, it may be made of wood or even plastic, yet it gives us better support than no chair leg at all.

This approach avoids the dissatisfaction caused by a neurotic search for "the perfect, the best, the absolutely greatest" and makes do with "good enough".

Major international companies, especially the big corporations, follow these principles. They diversify their investments and design experiments that risk the occasional failure, in the context of other more solid enterprises that will compensate for any weaknesses in the early stages. This offers the opportunity to assess the viability of the exercise providing at the same time the confidence to eliminate ventures that appear to be inauspicious or which might conflict with existing enterprises, hereby avoiding any conflict that might affect the overall good. These global plans take on board a constant element of uncertainty, the impact of which is minimized through the use of statistical forecasting, based on similar markets.

Progressing from the period of rigid Newtonian determinism, modern physics has studied this state of uncertainty, of random luck, in relation to the theory of chaos. There have been many attempts to harness mathematical formulae that have, since then, become part of the sophisticated calculations and equations used on a grand scale in Space Physics as well as at microcosmic levels in Nuclear Quantum Physics. Study of the economy has now assimilated this style of random chance calculation.

A multinational company, for example, will have interests in several markets, like oranges, shoes, cars, banking, art etc. As these markets fluctuate their revenue is cleverly shifted from one branch of the business to another and even if one branch is not thriving, the revenue can be held in waiting, "semi-dormant", waiting for better times. Otherwise a decision to close the branch has to be faced but the losses amortised by the many other more successful ventures.

In any good business, even when things are going very well, it is important to keep a close watch on the number of activities that it is possible to embrace with ease and effectiveness without causing stress to the leader whose job it is to maintain a proper balance between the initial intention to support and create new connections, and the capacity to carry these out.

It is not very different from the Malabar Plate Spinners who keep plates spinning in the air at the end of long sticks. If the plate spinner, wanting to make things even more difficult, starts to add more plates he needs to bring his attention back to the first set of plates in order to keep up the spinning speed and avoid the dangers of gravity making them fall to the ground. A little twist here, a little twist there and faster, faster, as he regulates the plates, all at once yet one at a time. A little twist in time avoids a disaster and the effort of having to go right back to the beginning and get them started all over again.

This image of the Malabar Plate Spinners brings with it the thought that at any given moment we may have to decide on a different course of action. To be over-ambitious in one's reach could risk the practical upkeep of existing personal resources which need to be protected in order to avoid undermining the basic supports.

These concepts explained through the previous metaphors can be related to practical therapy. When mental crises are dealt within a clinical environment, understanding the situation and focusing on tactics to resolve personal conflicts are not enough in themselves. In actual fact the capacity for understanding, the processing of walled-in conflicts from the past, the liberation of objectivity and emotional expression are all "legs" that help to reinforce a patient's personal suit of armour. But a strict awareness of other aspects on the periphery is to be advised, even if at first sight they don't appear to be related to the nub of the conflict. The therapist's job is to highlight these needs and help the patient extend his sources of support into every aspect of his life.

The metaphor that has been described, when appropriately applied, allows the therapist and the patient to regard the patient's mental health as his very own multinational business - adopting a multiple and varied perspective on sources of support, an essential dynamic, long term planning, learning to be flexible and to sacrifice branches of the business where necessary in order to benefit the enterprise as a whole. A business, for example, like the chair with many legs. Legs that move on wheels that are constantly changing. The wheel has a basic technology that allows for adaptation and mobility and is in itself a symbol of progress.

The business of survival in psychological life then becomes based upon projecting further than the individual himself towards an expanded reality and conscious integration of a network of social links that guarantee certain reciprocity. This is the perpetual bartering process which requires special attention over time in order to maintain the essence of mutual support which, if not nurtured, could disappear. This is the long-term stability one is seeking which, paradoxically never stands still and is never orderly. It has little stability, is predictably volatile, fluctuating and chaotic. It is dynamic, changeable, renewing and ultimately progressive.

Chapter 10

* * *

A WALK IN THE PARK

I f you walk down a city street with your headphones on your main
focus is on the tune that is being played. This music not only helps
keep out external noise but also tends to smooth away your worries.
When you turn the Walkman off you suddenly hear all sorts of new
sounds that you had not noticed before.

If your walk takes you somewhere where there is no traffic or city
bustle (in a park perhaps or in the countryside) you might find that the
birdsong becomes more evident or the rustle of the wind in the trees,
triggering different trains of thought. Should this all take place on a
clear summer's evening you could be transported into a calmer frame
of mind and with it an ever more subtle sequence of thoughts and emotions. Although you may be temped to attribute this feeling of calm in
the countryside to the surrounding silence, the experience it's not entirely devoid of noise. The silence, as it would appear, is relative when
compared with the noise of city traffic. This contrast creates a selec-
tive filter that allows certain sounds through, increasing the volume of

some and decreasing that of others thus encouraging to the surface ever more refined levels of sound.

The practice of psychotherapy is not far removed from this principle. The patient feels under pressure from his problems and unloads some of this in his encounter with the therapist. It is the receptive attitude of the therapist that allows the patient to shed some of his stress. The ability to listen without interference from any set agendas or personal pressure, without giving advice or offering any pre-conceived formulas as solutions, is the most effective approach. This ability to be receptive rests on the skills of the professional therapist who is able to maintain a state of mind that is calmer than that of the patient.

This receptivity is not exclusive to therapists. There are many instances in our relationships with friends and family and with our teachers when the mechanisms described above are reproduced.

If we analyse this process it may be that it has something to do with what the classicists called "nequaquam vacuum" meaning "there is no emptiness anywhere". It is as though nature abhors any kind of vacuum and needs to fill up any empty spaces immediately.

Silences in the midst of clinical dialogue create subtle gradients of pressure that maneuver patients towards experiences different to everyday ones. Previously guarded memories and images begin to surface in the immediate consciousness revealing traces of more profound and primitive thought patterns from the unconscious.

As this process is unpredictable, it can be accompanied by an increased level of fear and anxiety especially during those silences that the therapist has introduced and allows between the two of them.

The unconscious is ordered by means of a clever form of hierarchy just as the sounds during the walk in the park have their own order of precedence. These two, the unconscious and the park are examples of typical characteristics to be found in nature itself with its multiple layers and different densities.

The effects of these subtle gradients present themselves to the conscious mind and take it by surprise. It is as though the unmasking effect of the silences is experienced subjectively as a progressive sucking out of accumulated stress from both mind and body. A bit like an emotional vacuum cleaner – an extraction into emptiness!

There are those who are frightened by the thoughts that come bubbling up because they surface so quickly that the mind cannot assimilate them in an orderly or logical fashion so they appear to be incomprehensible. They can then be misinterpreted and, when certain basic defence mechanisms come into play, are rejected as being either too negative or too toxic. Some of these thoughts are replays of family situations that were rejected by the conscious mind a long time ago.

This process of discovery of the more subtle levels of consciousness can be as easy and pleasurable as the experience of walking through the park and hearing the birds singing and the wind rustling in the trees. It can also be as alarming as hearing the rumble of thunder of a rapidly approaching storm. However, avoiding these alarms is not always the best course of action. The walker might not have heard the first rumbles of thunder because the music playing through his headphones deprived him of the necessary information to take shelter from the storm in time.

This principle can equally work in reverse. The volume of the music in the headphones can be turned up on purpose in order to block

The principle is different. Every flow of communication requires an element of pressure gradient between the transmitter and the receptor. The emotional ventilation and the receptive, contemplative and meditative attitude encouraged by therapy or spiritual practice very often help to clear the mind and the heart of obsolete murkiness and channel personal potential to more realistic and ultimately more effective levels.

Chapter 11

✳   ✳   ✳

THE OLIVE TREE

O n a North East coastal seascape of Mallorca, in the municipality of Deiá, there's an ancient olive tree called "The Crocodile" after which the locality itself was named. This olive tree is nearly 700 years old. It is witness to many generations of children who climbed it and hung on its branches. Violent storms damaged its trunk. Its branches are hollowed out by inclement weather and eaten away by animals and insects as if the tree were their only sustenance. Today its trunk and its branches are twisted, but right at the top new branches appear with gleaming green leaves and occasional fruits.

I have used this image often in clinical practice. This tree's history symbolically echoes the history of many human beings who have endured hard and complicated lives, where fundamental problems early on in life have succeeded in distorting their personalities. These are people whose branches were sawn off in infancy by individuals close to them; sad, pain-inflicting family figures who have, in large part, gnawed away at the very essence of their victim's being. These victims have suffered traumatic events throughout their early life like, neglect, lack of affection, and a lack of care holding back and distorting their development.

Many people identify with the life of this old olive tree. They know instinctively what it is about. They also understand the tree's ability to survive and regenerate itself in the long term.

Although sometimes the tree may need pruning and tidying up, a good gardener, just to make the tree look beautiful, would never try to make the old severed branches grow again or attempt to straighten the trunk or fill in the holes with cement or smooth down the rough bark.

In the same way, the individual who identifies with the hardships of this tree learns painfully the futility of attempting to straighten out the sadness of the past, of hastily filling in the holes or cutting away at everything that appears unpleasant, ugly or humiliating. Any attempt at this will only serve to increase the woodworm and the rot, thus accelerating the tree's destruction.

The good gardener respects the past and learns to appreciate the tree's beauty and worth through the capricious shapes that have been honed by the passage of time. He will limit himself to protecting the tree from any misadventure and further deterioration. He might build a fence around it to keep animals and mischievous children away. He might give it suitable amounts of water avoiding soaking it.

The psychotherapist finds herself faced with a task similar to that of the gardener. Patients very often hope for and even expect a complete change, a re-structuring of their personality. They want to obliterate the past and to start with a clean slate. This expectation is so strong that it even seduces the clinician into wanting to help the patient beyond the patient's natural capacity. But like the gardener, chastened by the failure of several similar genuine attempts in the early enthusiasms of her career, she has learned to respect her limitations.

The therapist is now faced with the painful task of helping the patient accept more realistic goals. Painful because it is usually very difficult to let go of almost magical, instinctive beliefs in one's own powers or in the power of professionals to eradicate personal traits, beliefs, prejudices and other pre-conceived ideas. The prevailing culture of glamour that surrounds advances in medicine, the books that peddle cures and alternative transformations within a period of weeks, the wonder drugs and cosmetic surgery lead us to believe that anything is possible. Many patients have tried to fill their emptiness with drugs, alcohol, overwork, sexual promiscuity, escapist philosophies, burning the candle at both ends, only to find within a short space of time that the situation has become worse than before. Some have tried to eliminate the root pain by attempting suicide. In doing this they needlessly risk their lives. The truth is that their desperate attempts to end the pain have led them to confuse their target. Instead of aiming at their problems they aim at themselves.

The image of the centenarian tree carries with it a form of self-acceptance. This includes an acceptance of the past as it was, complete with its scars and the consequences of life's limitations. Those cavities, those traces of past losses, are the very ones that in their time nurtured the creative impulse. The gardener would never try to glue a fallen leaf back onto a branch in exactly the same position, rather he would trust in the ecological process of decomposition deep down in the earth and out of sight, to provide the necessary nutrients for the next phase, one that gives way to a new form of life, a new creation in another place.

In the same way, the therapist does not insist on the repetitive re-instatement of past losses, but instead allows entry of the basic compo-nents of her analysis into the terrain of the unconscious, confident in a future regeneration.

I have often invited the patient to imagine that he or she was the gardener responsible for this olive tree. I have asked them to consider the possibility of tearing the tree out because of its ugliness and use-lessness. Almost invariably the patient has responded that he would never do this to the tree. Patients appreciate its beauty and its valour. Adopting an ecological approach, they appreciate the tree in its original shape and value its intrinsic history. Just as the bonsai tree gardener values the trees that are the most gnarled and considers them to be the most beautiful.

This acceptance is rooted in the reality of the present. It casts aside any thoughts as what the tree would have been like if circumstances surrounding its growth had been more favourable. It clears away any expectations as to what it should have been like. Any grief for a past that never happened or for a future that was never going to be is tempered by this new perspective. This acceptance of the situation, such as it is, allows the person to rid himself of any self- deprecatory thoughts that might have existed under the hypnotic influence of remembered pain.

Therapy is not as simple as gardening. Working with acceptance does not presume a totally passive approach to the future. It is an ac-tivity that needs to be worked together with a personal sense of self-discipline and within the boundaries of a realistic landscape with goals that are attainable. It means focussing on the growth of the branches that remain. It means being more alert to the risks of falling back into the trap of seeking retribution or revenge for the pain of the past. Quite often the decomposing remains of the past need to be faced head on and this requires help from another human being. The desire to go back and mend the past from the position of the past acts like dangling a carrot in front of the donkey in terms of the human mind. It sucks insatiably at a person's energy.

The perspective achieved through auto-acceptance contributes to a solid recovery one where the patient has his feet on the ground. Just like the tree, for those who learn to appreciate it, it allows the discovery of a person's essential beauty and valour.

REFERENCES

1. Ainsworth, M.D.S., Blehar, M.C., Waters, E.& Wall, S. (1978). Patterns of attachment: A psychological study of strange situation. Hillsdale, N.J. Lawrence Erlbaum.

2. Albeniz, A (2012) Meeting YA in York, Systems Centred Journal, pp11-12, Vol 19 Number 1, Summer.

3. Bowlby, J:
   a) 1969 Attachment.London:Hogarth.1971 Harmondsworth:Pelican
   b) 1973 Separation, Anxiety and Anger. London:Hogarth.1975 Harmondsworth:Pelican
   c) 1980 Loss, sadness and Depression. London:Hogarth. 1981 Harmondsworth:Pelican.

4. DiClemente, C.C., Prochaska, J.O.,& Gilbertini, M. (1985). Self-efficacy and the stages of self-change in smoking. Cognitive Therapy and Research,9, pp 181-200.

5. Freud, S. (1912a/1958). The standard edition of the complete psychological works of Sigmund Freud. London: Hogarth Press.

6. Hilton, J (1933) Lost Horizon. Mass Market Paperback. Publisher: Pocket; edition 1945.

7. Jung, C.G. (1973) Memories, Dreams, Reflections, ed. Aniela Jaffe, transl. Richard and Clara Winston. New York: Pantheon Books.

8. Main, M.& Hesse, E. (1990) The insecure disorganised/ disoriented attachment pattern in infancy: Precursors and sequela. In M.T. Greeberg, D. Cichetti,& E.M.Cummings (Eds), Attachment in the preschool years: Theory, research and intervention (pp.161-182).Chicago: University of Chicago Press.

9. Payne, David S. (1992). Myth and Modern Man in Sherlock Holmes: Sir Arthur Conan Doyle and the Uses of Nostalgia. Bloomington, Ind: Gaslight's Publications.

10. Pérez-de Albeniz, A.J., Holmes, J.(1996).
    Review Article: Psychotherapy Integration, Its implications for Psychiatry.
    British Journal of Psychiatry, 169, pp 563-570.

11. Pérez-de-Albeniz, A.J., Holmes, J.(2000).
    Review Article: Meditation: Concepts, Effects and Uses in Therapy.The International Journal of Psychotherapy, 5,1, pp 49-58.

12. Pérez-de-Albeniz, A.J. (2006).
Review article: Psychological Aspects of Looking after Dying People. Quarterly Journal of Mental Health,1,2, pp 44-49.

13. Vaillant, GE.(1992).
Ego Mechanisms of Defence: a guide for clinicians and researchers. Washington:American Psychiatric Association.

14. Winnicott DW(1965). The maturational Processes and the Facilitating Enviroment:Studies in the Theory of Emotional development. London:Hogarth Press.

✳ ✳ ✳
ABOUT THE AUTHOR

Dr. Alberto Albeniz grew up and studied medicine in Spain. He moved to the United Kingdom in 1989 to work and train with the National Health Service.

Dr. Albeniz became a member of the Royal College of Psychiatrists in 1995. He specialized as a consultant psychiatrist in psychotherapy and became a member of the Institute of Group Analysis in 2000.

Over the past ten years, Dr. Albeniz has led a community treatment unit of people who suffer from personality disorders. He combines group and individual psychotherapy within a psychiatric framework in Coventry. He also serves as a psychotherapy tutor in the West Midlands, teaching and supervising psychiatric trainees, psychologists, psychotherapists, nurses, and social workers

Contact e-mail: zin2per@gmail.com

19299331R00063

Printed in Great Britain
by Amazon